T0267034

SAVAGE TALES

Tara Bergin is an Irish poet. Her first collection, *This is Yarrow* (2013), won the Seamus Heaney Prize for Poetry, and the Shine/Strong Award for best first collection by an Irish author. She received an Arts Council Ireland Literature Bursary to write her second collection, *The Tragic Death of Eleanor Marx* (2017), which was shortlisted for the T.S. Eliot and Forward Prizes, and chosen as Best Poetry Book of the year by *The Times* and *The Irish Times*. She now lives in the North of England.

SAVAGE TALES

TARA BERGIN

CARCANET POETRY

First published in Great Britain in 2022 by
Carcanet
Alliance House, 30 Cross Street
Manchester, M2 7AQ
www.carcanet.co.uk

A CIP catalogue record for this book is
available from the British Library.

ISBN 978 1 80017 231 9

Front cover and final illustration: © The Disposable Museum Collective
Book design by Andrew Latimer
Printed in Great Britain by SRP Ltd, Exeter, Devon

The publisher acknowledges financial
assistance from Arts Council England.

CONTENTS

II
CAMPUS POEMS

V

THE SLEEP AND DREAM NOTEBOOKS

VI
WOLF FABLES

VII
THE BLACKBIRD DIARIES

To my beautiful friend

I

THE ARTIST AND HIS [SIC] WORK

Tell me, he said, when our paths crossed on the green. Do they call you a poetess?
Oh, I said. They don't use that word any more.

The Subject Field

I crawl on my hands and knees to my notebook.

The Crisis

The barman had a dog-eared copy of *Japanese Death Poems*
underneath the counter.
A bit of light reading? I said.
Did you want to order something? he said.

Japanese Death Poem

In the second state I strike through the first state and sign again correctly. In the third state I erase the whole thing. That's what April was like this year. Very torn up.

April Dogs

Oh Rose, I said to myself as I unlocked my bike, Thou art sick. Then I rode into the stinking traffic feeling comparatively cheerful.

Blake's Rose

If you're wondering why you never feature in your mother's or father's memories, said the doctor pushing himself over to the computer and beginning to type, the answer is pretty straightforward. You are nowhere to be found in their happy childhoods, their difficult teenage years, or their joyful life together as a young couple. He turned to me and smiled brightly. Nothing serious!

The Stranger

The eye is an aperture. The lid is bone. You can't ask it any questions. The tongue is stone.

Self Portrait in a Bad Year

Sometimes it's not helpful to see the street as a place full of secrets waiting to be fathomed.

The Curb

We get a lot of writers in here, said the optician tightening
the screws.

The Optician

Queued for bread today. No one standing in the line whispered in my ear through blue lips: Can you write about this? If they had, I would have said: I can't.

Not Anna Akhmatova

Look, she said, lowering her voice. There are three ways this can go: Done to you. Letting it be done to you. Doing it yourself. Which one's it going to be?

The Actor

I have never thought of myself as one of the girls: coarse fishing, lamping, heavyweight boxing; these are the topics I tend to raise in conversation.

Difficulties arise because I have little (if any) direct experience of such activities.

The Girls

We get a lot of writers in here, said the rollercoaster operator lowering the bar.

The Rollercoaster Operator

A.

You said that ever since last Sunday you had been feeling an acute pain, not dissimilar to remorse, and I thought perhaps we could begin there.

B.

With the pain?

A.

With the remorse.

Session Three: Public Appearances

What we want, said the Manager, is to sound like we're all on the same level. Do you know what I mean? Do you think you are the person who can help us do that?

Oh yes, I think so, judging by my previous experience. In my last position the idea was to start with something human, to make it sound like we're all on the same level.

That, said the Manager, is exactly what we want.

Line Manager

If only there were a drop for the tongue – something bitter and strong to be taken at night and in the morning for seven days. Or a new way of breathing.

The Sickness

When leaving for breakfast in the morning I saw a small amount of hope had been left just outside my door. I took it downstairs to the receptionist. 'I didn't order this.'

Room Service

The artist does not work for money but for his [sic] art.

The Artist

At one end – lead. At the other – rubber.

Whatever may flower I quickly devour.

The Pencil

Ibsen: We are thoughts. You should have thought us. You should have given us little feet.

Lines from Peer Gynt

Joyce: I am a young Irishman, eighteen years old, and the words of Ibsen I shall keep in my heart all my life.

Letter to Ibsen's Translator

I can say EVERYTHING if it can be smuggled inside something else.

The Fabulist

Nietzsche: Are you genuine? Or just a play-actor?

I speak to myself like a dog owner speaks to its dog. Leave it, I warn myself. Drop it!

The Bite

Robbing Peter to pay Paul is a dangerous practice with many risks but because of its potential benefits I continue to take my chances.

Bankruptcy

At 4 a.m. I speak to myself like a judge to the witness: just answer the question.

The Trial

I say that I want the truth but what I actually want is for your lying technique to improve.

The Lie

We get a lot of writers in here, said the wine taster spitting in a bowl.

The Wine Taster

Warning: You are about to enter a courtroom in which the recording equipment is very sensitive. Even when speaking very quietly you will be recorded.

The Courtroom

Felicity to Mary: What's your deepest fear?
Mary: Homelessness.
Felicity: Everyone says that.

Your Fear

I experience 'the fragment' as if it were a dramatic moment in a play (the ex-lover enters after eight years of absence and everything shatters).

The Gasp

De Chirico: Close your eyes and see.

De Chirico's Vision

When you step over the letter 'I' you enter into the black woods of prophecy: a hundred eyes.

The Ninth Letter

I notice your boots because I am at ground level.

The Gutter

If pushed I would say I dislike the double negative.

Not Unusual

When Baudelaire compares a woman's hair to petrol and wild grasses and salt I feel better.

Baudelaire's Hair

I tell the dentist: My mouth is blind.
What do you mean blind?
I gave my eyeteeth to jealousy.

The Confession

All I could think about while I sat in the operating chair was the Anna Magdalena notebooks.

The Excoriation

The sound of car wheels on the gravel drive turned out to be hailstones on the window.

The Hailstorm

The sound of next door banging the wall turned out to be snow falling from the porch roof.

The Snowstorm

On the drive home the feeling in my mouth started to come back.

The Thaw

II
CAMPUS POEMS

You at the front, I said pointing to a student with their hand up.
Yeah I just wanted to ask, what exactly is a Campus Poem?
I nodded and smiled demonstrably just like the instruction
manual had shown me.
Great question, I said. What *is* a Campus Poem?
Several of the students raised their hands, so I let them kill two
birds with one stone.

You at the Front

What author would you pick as an example in your talk about identity? Remember there are no wrong answers. Even so, the candidate managed to give the wrong answer.

The Panel

When I started I thought the one who wore black was the philosopher but the philosopher was on the other side and always wore white.

The Doors

You will have to say: *I* was beaten. *My* child was taken away from me.

Interpretation Training

In the film *Taxi Driver* we see the city through a taxi driver's windscreen. Indeed much of the film's power is due to this limited perspective.

Every year I use this as an example even though the students have never heard of *Taxi Driver*.

I tell the students that etymologically speaking, the word 'conceive' does not mean 'to make' but 'to take'.

Creative Practice

Akhmatova: These things are half-stolen.

Poem Without a Hero

When William Carlos Williams said 'don't blush to write a poem' did he mean we should open up or close down?

Blushing to Write This

During the lecture on 'working practices' I made sure to speak only in the second person. Even so the whole time I was talking my face was very hot.

Working Practice

During the Q&A following the lecture on working practices I made sure to speak only in the third person. Even so the whole time my hands were very animated.

Q&A

The hanged man in a tree.
The firing squad.
These are among the earliest examples of etching being used
to communicate the ravages of war.

The Hanged Man

'Engulfment'. 'Implosion'. 'Petrification'. A writer without words is desperate.

The Divided Self

All hands fall into three classes. The hand of the soldier. The hand of the philosopher. The hand of the dreamer.

All Hands Fall

There is always the double-edged worry that we are missing something of significance or over-interpreting what we see.

The Sword

You at the back, I said pointing to a student with their hand up.
Yeah I just wanted to ask, what are Night Terrors?
I nodded and smiled demonstrably just like the instruction
manual had shown me.
Great question, I said. What *are* Night Terrors?
Several of the students raised their hands, so I let them
experience it for themselves.

You at the Back

For maximum effect, says Henri Bergson, the comic demands something like a momentary anaesthesia of the heart.

Comedy and Tragedy

O to break free of the Master –
to strike through the first person – to reach at all costs the
second or third –

My Master's Thesis

Headline: Short sentences prove that prisons don't work.

Sentencing

In one person: nine characters.

Character Count

Okay everybody, here is the algorithm. Eight or lower gives a zero. Nine or higher gives a one. This should give us the results we want. If not, don't worry. I can write a different algorithm.

End of Year Breakdown

If you're going to have eyes at the end you should have them running all the way through.

Feedback on Eyes

Don't say 'working class'. Say 'low budget'.

Class Feedback

Here's what my dictionary tells me about concrete: it's real.

On the Use of Specifics

III
THE NEW ROMANTICS

The seduction: If I fall in love with you I'll kill myself.

Success

The nervous man: What colour is your black bike?

Failure

Laying out his little clay hearts the potter said: They will all harden soon.

The Pessimist

We can do it contactlessly if you want.

New Advances

Freud: Men scatter small change and in that way pay whatever fee they think appropriate for the session.

Now the pitch is split in half into the 'attack zone' and the 'defensive zone'.

Two Zones

Called Gregorio in error.

Postcard from the Library

I never wanted to be your weekday lover.

Girl Friday

In hindsight it strikes me as odd that when X mistook my tenderness for sadism I didn't think 'he's misunderstood me' but rather 'he's seen something I didn't know was there'.

Penetration

'That was my era,' I say confidently, 'the New Romantics,' even though it's nothing to be proud of.

My Era

Romantic: I wandered lonely.

New Romantic: I only want to see you dancing in the purple rain.

Somebody took a photograph of Prince leaving a pharmacy in Minnesota. It's a poor quality picture – a low resolution shot of a man dressed in black – but it has a very high value because of what happened next.

Prince at the Chemist

I kept saying I can't bear to leave the Amelanchier Lamarkii, the Concord Pear, the Annie Elizabeths, but what I really meant was I can't bear to leave the mountain.

Me and the Mountain

When Milena appeared in Kafka's dream they kept merging into each other. Finally she somehow caught fire but then transmutability entered and it was Kafka who was on fire.

Dream of Milena

Flashover: When the fire inside a room becomes a room on fire.

Lovestory

There'd been some bullying but it was only when he pawned my engagement and wedding rings that I woke up and thought: This isn't love.

Coercive Cohesive

While reading his journal my first thought was to try to be like the 'small woman ready for anything' that X hankered after. Then I remembered.

Bad Reaction

Pull the other close to you, put your forehead on their shoulder and hold tight while leaning with as much of your weight towards them as possible.

Use the element of surprise.

The Clinch as a Tactic

When you lean in try to push your head consistently and firmly on the other's collarbone.

If done correctly this can turn the whole game around.

The Clinch for Survival

Be confident and remember you can escape a clinch with several moves.

Just keep in mind which hand is the leading one.

Escaping the Clinch

IV
STRANGE NEWS

Savagery in the fields again: the white flesh of the hawthorns torn and exposed; limbs strewn at their feet.

Field Notes

I had two tortures last week alone.

Woman's Hour

I never listen to the radio, says the young woman scalding my scalp. How does that feel?

Dead Ends

When the removal van knocked down our back wall I went round to ask what they were going to do about it. They didn't apologise and I left saying 'Thank you'.

Logistics

I showed it to him. He liked it. He took it and used it. Now I want it back.

Colony

I said: It's the hot tap, it screams when you turn it on.
She said: Every time? Every time you turn it on it screams?
And I said: Yes every time.
So she said: Send me a photograph of the tap itself – I
already know what the scream looks like – and we'll try to
get somebody out.

Loose Reviver

When everything was over she took me aside and showed me a bear's paw that she had wrapped in a scarf in her handbag.

Is it yours? she said. My daughter says it must be. We think you left it in the café.

I wasn't in the café, I said. I didn't even know they had one.

The Claw

For the party I baked little cakes and decorated them with paper butterflies. You can eat the butterflies, I told the kids, but they hesitated. Eat them! I said. They taste like Christ tasted when I was your age.

Edible Paper

I wish I was the sort of person who didn't wish they were a different person.

The Condition

In Nolde's painting the twelve year old Christ stands, leans on his arms, head down, adults tell him he has to do it, he is chosen, etc. etc. The child is nicely painted. The adults look like puppets.

'This is now a discredited Social Darwinist position.'

Nolde's Christ

Some people are tenants and some people are landlords.

Landlord: The landlord rules, not the tenant. I think you've worked that out, haven't you?

Me to the landlord: You need to come over. I'm sleeping alongside rats.

The landlord's wife: We all have to do it some time in our lives.

Tenants and Landlords

A quick check of the dictionary confirms it. 'To shrive' means 'to absolve' but it can also mean 'to be absolved.' Only context will help us from here.

Pancake Tuesday

When X recounts happy childhood memories he speaks in the second person as if they were my memories.

Perspective

The bus pulls up and the doors open. On clamber the philosophers in their black eye makeup. The mothers and toddlers wait behind. The toddlers wave goodbye to the bus's windows with padded gloves. One calls hello! by mistake. They still know nothing of separation. The bus moves off and all the mothers break apart.

The School Bus

While the ferry is docking do not hold your children in your arms.

Safety Warning, Staten Island

Out walking by the river I become irritable with everyone's chatter as if they're talking in the cinema. What's that called?

An Outing

Tsvetaeva: I'm so and so, the wife of my husband and the mother of my children.

October 1917

X to the pain: You can go, I won't mind.

Polite Notice

The mother: a complicated field of dreams; electrified fences; locked gates; gaps; blackthorn bushes.

Matrix

When I was drowning everything was white even the tips of my fingers.

When I was saved everything was green even the cone of the larch tree.

The White Winter and the Green Winter

Now the kittens have grown a little, X has started to take them outside, kneeling on the ground and speaking to them in a high voice, patting the grass to invite them to play like you do with very young children when they're starting to walk.

Toddlers

The date on the coin (a three kopek piece) is 1880. Chekhov is starting to write.

Historical Present

When I was young I spoke of imminent resolution in the pure happiness of C major. Now I speak of the most gloomy condition of the soul in the key of D sharp minor.

'If ghosts could speak, their speech would approximate this key.'

Key Characteristics

Things seem to slip from my fingers a lot these days. This morning: the white ramekin. Yesterday: my mother's eyes.

Slipping

Bois does not mean 'wood' but the smell of the wood, just as *lapin* does not mean rabbit but the troubled boy's only friend.

Direct Line

I remember my daughter's flowering rosary. It bloomed one flower a day for ten days and then stopped: a Holy Mary Mother of God for only two working weeks. Could the panel tell me why this happened and how we get it to flower again for longer?

Favour

Chekhov used to stand at the window of his study in Yalta and look through binoculars at the town and the sea beyond – he saw everything very close up, while remaining at a distance.

I didn't think of that myself.

Chekhov's Binoculars

Dostoevsky describing the drowning woman: Her skirt whipped up ballooning on the surface like a pillow.

The Drowning Woman

Dostoevsky describing Raskolnikov: He was in a kind of black ecstasy.

The Drowning Man

The dictionary of Christian lore and legend: 'The Seven Joys of Mary' cf. 'The Seven Sorrows of Mary'.

Motherhood

Rilke in Paris: The mould-maker I pass every day has put out two masks by his door. The face of the young woman who drowned and beneath it his own knowing face.

Rilke's Masks

White ground: instruction for preparing a woodblock.

It could also be a description of the winter streets today.

Block 1: The aesthetics of nature

What You Will Study

V

THE SLEEP AND DREAM NOTEBOOKS

Someone had smashed the door of the studio and taken everything. It should have been my dream not his.

The Break In

Hopkins: I wake and feel the fell of dark not day.

Morning Prayer

Last night: one or two touches of the afterlife; like the branches of ivy that creep into the gap in the shed wall and touch a different existence. The dead say ordinary things and everyone is happy with that.

The Visits

You are the quail of day in the mouth of night.

Night Feeding

At some point in the middle of the night the rose that gave honey to the bees fell apart and scattered its ashes beneath my window.

I never even woke up.

Night Rose

When my aunt answered the phone with my grandmother's voice I was transported.

Time Travel

Oh phone call. I'm going to dream about you.

After Mandelstam

Door slamming. Car engine. Car driving away. I close my eyes and dream about opening my eyes.

Daily Rituals

All night, visions of the gallows. Half-dreams of an 'execution site'. Who was going to hang their head? So keen to get an answer I didn't stop to listen. A pen with a light so I could write in the dark. A page full of pauses and dashes. Heat. Cold. Alarm.

Night Visions

Yesterday woke with this word: execution. Today: assassination.

Surfaces and Depths

In the middle of the night downstairs in the grate the coal and ashes had reformed and were in flames. 'Put your money where your mouth is.'

Night Sacrifice

Dream: The butcher kisses me on the lips and takes me by surprise. Reality: He stands among the carcasses which are bone and flesh.

Dream vs Reality

Swoons. Apoplexy. Burns and scalds. Catalepsy. Epilepsy.
Vibrations of the throat and eye.

Dream Notebook

Every night I die and am buried.

Every morning I am reborn good as new.

Current Routine

At night I divide
My hair
And plait each side
Before I sleep.

My hair is very long.

The plaits grip my head
Like teeth.

VI
WOLF FABLES

The wolf watches through the fence how the farmer chooses, kills, and guts one of the sheep. He looks at the dogs sleeping quietly in the yard. They don't even care, thinks the wolf leaving in annoyance.

The Psychotic is the name we have for the other person.

Wolf and Shepherds

When I was stroking his foot I saw that the base of his foot –
its palm – was black with dirt. This was of course a swapping
around. It was my foot and he was stroking it.

Wolf and Psychiatrist

Sometimes the truth is more bearable when it is only half-open. (That's how the story of cruelty began).

Wolf and Fox

When the wolf runs from the forest into the village it is not for a visit. He needs to save himself because his behavioural skin is trembling. He no longer feels substantial. He looks for an opening but all the gates are closed.

The wolf sees a cat sitting on the fence. Vassenka! calls the wolf. Where can I hide from those vicious dogs?

What dogs? says the cat. I don't hear any dogs.

I do, says the wolf. They are tearing me apart.

Wolf and Cat

You watch the others spit on their paws; you see them hide their bad breath; you can't move with them or away from them.

The only way to survive is to talk to yourself.

As if you were the second person.

The Split

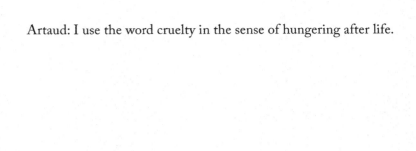

Artaud: I use the word cruelty in the sense of hungering after life.

Letters of Cruelty

All wolves have long legs, a triangular head, triangular ears, a bushy tail. In some countries the wolf becomes a fellow hunter but once you domesticate them they become thieves.

No I-Thou Relationship

In the shape of a wolf, Struwwelpeter trespasses.

Slovenly Peter

The wolf is the inner self that we can't suppress.

I am stroking the wolf.

I want to be frightened.

Wolf Love

Little Red Cap: Oh my God how frightened I feel today.

Fairy Tale

In Franz Marc's *Birth of the Wolf* the wolf is hidden to the lower right side like the pain in the abdomen. The branches and thorns grow upwards into a pyramid: a thicket. Some light. Some darkness. The father is out. There is danger in the distance.

Franz Marc's Lair

No shadow-puppets in the cave of the Wolf Zeus. No Platonic understanding of human perception. You forget everything within a year.

Wolf Zeus

One night while the wolf was sleeping the sheep gathered together to carry out a plan. They crept into the lair, stole the wolf's eyes, and stuck them onto his back legs. Then they crept away without the wolf even moving a muscle.

In the morning the wolf killed the sheep as usual.

But for once he saw the damage he'd done in hindsight.

Wolf and Eyes

VII
THE BLACKBIRD DIARIES

This could change my whole life I thought when I heard the first few notes of the harmonium.

Overreaction

When I look in the oval mirror in the hall I see only my mother and myself. I don't see the 'evaluated' one. She must be in the third person.

I spend so long looking the glass blushes and the dinner gets cold.

Two Dimensions

The mirror: a controlling God; a jealous God.

The Mirror God

Do you look at yourself in the mirror? I often look at myself in the small mirror in the living room. Still no sign of the formal 'you' anywhere.

French Lessons

Today the oval mirror is covered by a black cloth. It's not for mourning; it's the washing hanging up to dry. Either way it's a relief not to see that grey-haired woman every time I go up the stairs.

The Burden of the Mirrors

In a moment, the forget-me-not. But first, the intoxicating rose.

Offerings

On his last day visiting the hawthorns: I promise that when I grow up...

Proust's Vow

Overcast. The blackbird's chosen a different tree this morning.

Dull Day

Yesterday I was all eyes. Today, blind.

The White Page

Jules Renard calls the blackbird a minuscule crow but that's to overlook its most remarkable feature.

Jules Renard's Comparison

Free, then borrowed, then stolen time.

Three Stages

I used to listen to the news in the morning but now I listen to the blackbird.

The Messages

This day last week: 'violently ill'. Today: 'happy because no longer violently ill.'

Logic

Too wet this morning to translate the blackbird.

No Signal

The child's tree: prismatic. Like a rod that stands between two bands.

A warm late summer breeze in the last days of August blows the hawthorn's thick leaves away from its face.

Too many adjectives but how to let go?

A breeze in August parts my mother's hair.

Easterly

VIII
FOUR DANCES

I was wearing my blue 1940s swimsuit and high heeled shoes
and my hair was loose and long and beautiful very dark like
my mother's. I had just lifted the heavy dining room table
and carried it across the room when the telephone rang.
It was my mother who said she could come round later to
help. I don't need your help or anyone else's I shouted and
slammed down the phone. Afterwards I counted the fingers
on my left hand: FIVE. A whole hand and wrist and arm to
use as I wished.

Same on the other side.

The Waltz

First my right hand opened through my left hand. Then my right hand touched my forehead. Then my right hand fell downwards like a leaf. Then I made two fists and held them up in the air. Now I have lived a whole life.

The Seasons Dance

I was pretty shy when I started and then one day my mother called me and said you have to get crazier. That was the only advice she gave me in twenty years. So next time I put on a long black dress with red hearts and a pair of very high heels and allowed my whole body to fall forward like a tree. My face was nearly touching the grass before someone bent down and caught me. My hair was long and very beautiful very dark like my mother's.

I did this dance many times and everybody loved it.

The Fall Dance

I was wearing my long pink satin dress and high-heeled shoes and I was standing in the middle of a room. All the men had to fight their way through to stroke my hair, touch my face, prod my stomach and pluck the skin around my collarbone. They lifted me up and shook me to see if anything would fall out. When they slapped me it was like you might slap the rump of an animal. At some point I'm not sure exactly when all the men went away.

It's hard to remember.

The Inspection Dance

IX
CONSTRUCTIONS

Ovid–19

This is the letter of ex   isle

I want to be with you any way I can

All of the   neighbours   have learned my name

I want to be with you

I'll die of nostalgia   & so will the kids

I want to be with you any way I can

storm   to rose   to blood   to storm   12 moons

I want to be

Why write   you ask   these letters

I've told you

Blue Hydrangea

The philosophical tongue of the soil is not acidic enough to whip these flowers into a state of self-hatred.

They won't bloom into Proust's dead turquoise.

They won't be cut by Blanche's knife and placed in the hand of a sentimental child.

Too aware of their own reality they can't indulge Gallé's anthropomorphic fantasies: no blue melancholy; no wilting neurasthenic blue.

Montesquiou's blue wreath won't have them: his muse won't even dream of them.

They will not open into the faded blue of Rilke's writing paper.

Because of this they will not be placed in the service of a new aesthetic.

They can never be blue.

Unless the tongue of the earth becomes ruder, meaner.

Two Judiths

The first Judith wants it   the second Judith suffers from it.

The first Judith dresses up for it   the second Judith is left exposed by it.

The first Judith stares at it   the second Judith can't face it.

The first Judith is hungry   and makes us hungry for it.

The second Judith is sickened by it   and we fear the second.

The first Judith grabs the head   and pushes it down.

The second Judith prepares a speech   and holds it up.

She holds it up dripping   before the people of Need City.

Weird Sister

I wrote out Ruth in the afternoon – Dorothy Wordsworth

We
were a
triangle –
three figures tied
by imaginary lines; three
points never in an ordinary row
together;
eternal triangle; Wm upon my breast
and I upon Mary; a triangle of forces –
held in equilibrium – sounded by striking with a rod:
call me not *Naomi* –
call me a frame of three halberds joined at the top
to which a soldier is bound for flogging; call me the three
stars north of *Aries*; call me a sailor, a beggar, a mantua-maker;
call me three quarrels...three complaints:
when he kissed me his mouth and breath were very cold;
no little birds, no thrushes; call me –
three persons; three corners: the blind man and his wife and sister
sitting by the fire   all dressed very clean in their Sunday clothes.

Object Theory

The found object is a lesson in metaphor.
It is found then named e.g. the fountain.
It is shifted to a context where it evokes new meanings.

next slide please

The found object hungers after life. It seeks out positional truth.
It must not break away from danger.

next slide please

The open eye. The iron mouth. The breakable cheekbone.

next slide please

The artist builds a little chamber. Light is admitted through a tiny hole.
Everything you see will be upside down.

Quartz

Say you take a piece of quartz found on a building site on the side of a road and you put it on a sheet of paper on the windowsill on a sunny morning during the Holidays. Not yours, theirs. Say There's Nothing to Do. They say that not you. Say it's warm because of the sun yet cold in spite of it. Say your own soul is dark like the coal in the hod. Or like the soot at the foot of the coal bunker the soul no one sees but the disappointed shovel. Okay say the coal man knows but he never dwells he has raised his status where you retained yours. Say you take the magnifying glass and look through it at the quartz and say you see it shine and say it blinds the soul that bothers you pulls at your hem. Say it is a spotlight onto your good side. Say it warms your cockles and mussels and makes you put them in a barrow. Wheel them like babes by the light-filled river and sing them away. Say you're a this, say you're a that. Say the light dazzles distracts you from your own complications. Shines or blinds the self out of itself like cauterising a wound. Say cauterize. Say sear. Say Hot. Iron. Pleasing for it do be old-fashioned. Today a blood blister. Tomorrow I eat from your spoon. What next, if we already share spit and injury? Say Blame. Say Hope. Say it in the cold dark of day so that your breath crystalises and I can pluck it and wear it as a Brooch. Say it: No one wears Brooches anymore.

ACKNOWLEDGEMENTS

Thanks are due to the editors of the following publications in which some of these pieces first appeared, sometimes in slightly different forms: *Evergreen Review*, *Granta*, *The Idler*, *Poetry London*, *The Poetry Review* (first in Anna Woodford's essay on 'The Campus Poem' and then in the Spring 2022 issue); *PN Review*, *Prototype*, *Winter Papers*.

'Object Theory' was commissioned by The Model, Sligo, in response to Marie Foley's Portrait. 'Weird Sister' was commissioned by Unlaunched Books. 'Quartz' was commissioned by BBC Radio 3's *The Verb* for their Freethinking Festival at Gateshead.

The 'Four Dances' were written in response to works by Pina Bausch.

CONSTRUCTION

poetry is not a sport it is a spectacle.

The function of poets is not to win; it is to go through

the emotions expected of them.

The virtue of all-in poetry is that it is the spectacle of excess.

In poetry a man who is down is exaggeratedly so.

In poetry one is not ashamed of one's suffering.

Poetry is diacritical writing: above one meaning another is placed.

What the public wants is the image of passion not passion itself.

What is at stake is the triumph of pride and the formal concern

with truth.

In poetry defeat is not an outcome it is a duration.

What is portrayed in poetry is an ideal understanding of things.

In poetry nothing exists except the absolute.

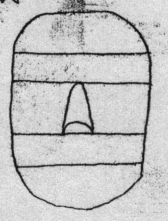